A DAY IN THE LIFE OF A DOCTOR

THIS EDITION
Produced for DK by WonderLab Group LLC
Jennifer Emmett, Erica Green, Kate Hale, *Founders*

Editor Maya Myers; **Photography Editor** Kelley Miller; **Managing Editor** Rachel Houghton;
Designers Project Design Company; **Researcher** Michelle Harris; **Copy Editor** Lori Merritt;
Indexer Connie Binder; **Proofreader** Susan K. Hom; **Series Reading Specialist** Dr. Jennifer Albro

First American Edition, 2025
Published in the United States by DK Publishing, a division of Penguin Random House LLC
1745 Broadway, 20th Floor, New York, NY 10019

Copyright © 2025 Dorling Kindersley Limited
24 25 26 27 10 9 8 7 6 5 4 3 2 1
001-345391-April/2025

All rights reserved.
Without limiting the rights under the copyright reserved above, no part of this publication may be reproduced, stored in or introduced into a retrieval system, or transmitted, in any form, or by any means (electronic, mechanical, photocopying, recording, or otherwise), without the prior written permission of the copyright owner.
Published in Great Britain by Dorling Kindersley Limited

A catalog record for this book is available from the Library of Congress.
HC ISBN: 978-0-5939-6233-6
PB ISBN: 978-0-5939-6232-9

DK books are available at special discounts when purchased in bulk for sales promotions, premiums, fund-raising, or educational use. For details, contact:
DK Publishing Special Markets, 1745 Broadway, 20th Floor, New York, NY 10019
SpecialSales@dk.com

Printed and bound in China
Super Readers Lexile® levels 310L to 490L
Lexile® is the registered trademark of MetaMetrics, Inc. Copyright © 2024 MetaMetrics, Inc. All rights reserved.

The publisher would like to thank the following for their kind permission to reproduce their images:
a=above; c=center; b=below; l=left; r=right; t=top; b/g=background
123RF.com: Choreograph 30bl; **Dreamstime.com:** 18percentgrey 27cr, 30cla, Yuri Arcurs 19tl, 29cb, Erol Demir 24, Imagesupply 20-21, Paul-andré Belle-isle 18cr, Jovanmandic 9, 30cl, Viktor Levi 4-5, 14-15t, Rudra Narayan Mitra 12-13, Monkey Business Images 6-7, 11c, 30clb, Tyler Olson 7c, Prostockstudio 1, Sofiia Shunkina 26, 30tl, Sjors737 18t, Wanuttapong Suwannasilp 19bl, Bongkarn Thanyakij 29c, Wavebreakmedia Ltd 3; **Getty Images:** Anadolu 17, Massimo Di Nonno 16; **Getty Images / iStock:** E+ / Andresr 22, E+ / AsiaVision 12-13bc, E+ / Bymuratdeniz 19cb, E+ / FatCamera 25, E+ / Fstop123 23, E+ / SDI Productions 15ca, E+ / Shapecharge 27t, Gorodenkoff 28-29, Maleraspaso 19cr, Martinns 8, Realpictures 10, XiXinXing 19cr, Drazen Zigic 7cb; **Shutterstock.com:** Dragana Gordic 11t

Cover images: *Front:* **Dreamstime.com:** Nataliia Darmoroz (Background), Wavebreakmedia Ltd;
Back: **Dreamstime.com:** Zuper_Electracat cra, Anatolii Riabokon clb

www.dk.com

This book was made with Forest Stewardship Council™ certified paper – one small step in DK's commitment to a sustainable future. Learn more at www.dk.com/uk/information/sustainability

Level 1

A DAY IN THE LIFE OF A
DOCTOR

Paige Towler

Contents

6	Meet a Doctor
10	Getting Ready
12	At Work
20	Teamwork
22	Staying Healthy

28 A Long Day
30 Glossary
31 Index
32 Quiz

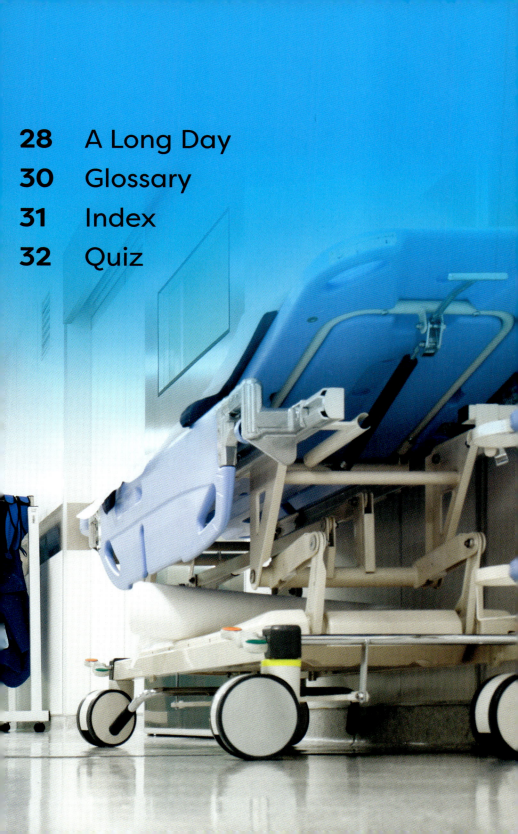

Meet a Doctor

Not feeling good? It might be time to see a doctor.

Doctors help people get better when they are sick or hurt.

Doctors also help people stay healthy.

There are many different kinds of doctors.
Some doctors treat just one part of the body.
Some doctors only take care of children.
The people a doctor takes care of are called patients.

This doctor is a primary care doctor. She gets to know her patients well. She keeps track of their health.

Getting Ready

This doctor wears regular work clothes. He wears a white coat. The coat has pockets for his tools.

These doctors wear scrubs. Scrubs are comfortable. They are easy to move in. They are also easy to clean.

At Work

Some doctors work at a clinic. A clinic is a doctor's office.

Some people come when they feel sick. The doctor tries to figure out what's wrong.

Some people just need a checkup.

Doctors see lots of patients every day. Sometimes, they help patients over a call.

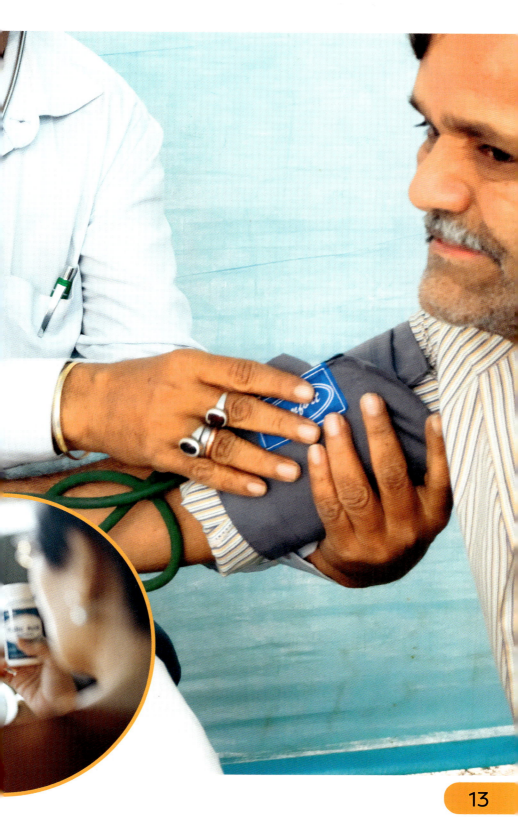

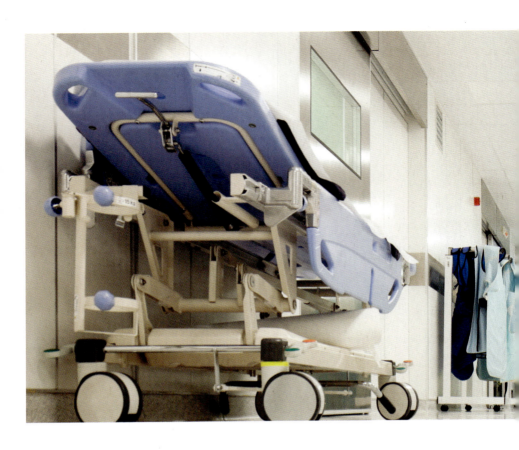

Some doctors work at a hospital. People who are sick or hurt can go to a hospital. Doctors and nurses work there all day and all night. They take care of people.

This baby was just born. The doctor checks on the baby.

A doctor visits each patient. This is called doing rounds.

Sometimes, there are emergencies. They can happen in places with no hospitals. Doctors travel to these places. They set up field hospitals and clinics. They take care of people who need help.

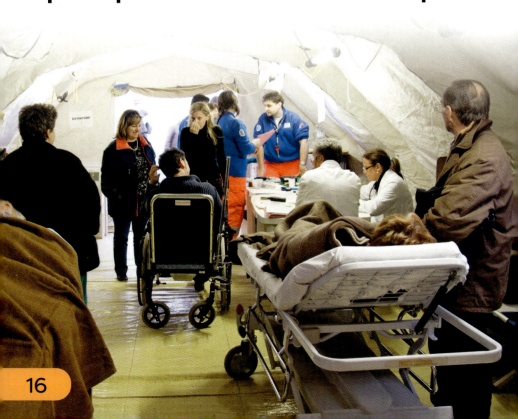

Other doctors travel from place to place. They use mobile hospitals. They take care of people wherever they go.

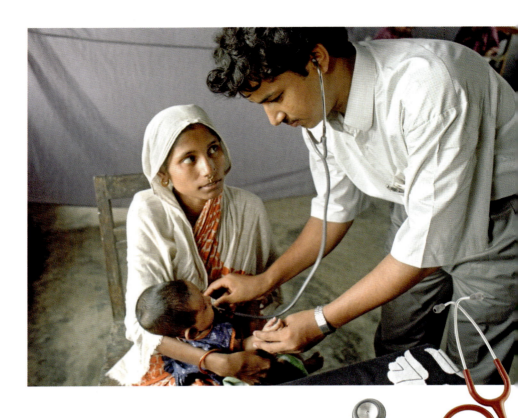

Doctors use tools. A stethoscope lets the doctor hear a person's heart beating. The doctor listens to the person's lungs, too.

Doctors also use other tools.

thermometer: measures a person's temperature

blood pressure cuff: measures how a person's blood is pumping

otoscope: lets a doctor see inside a person's ears

tongue depressor: lets a doctor see down a person's throat

Teamwork

It is a lot of work to keep people healthy!

Doctors work with nurses and other doctors.

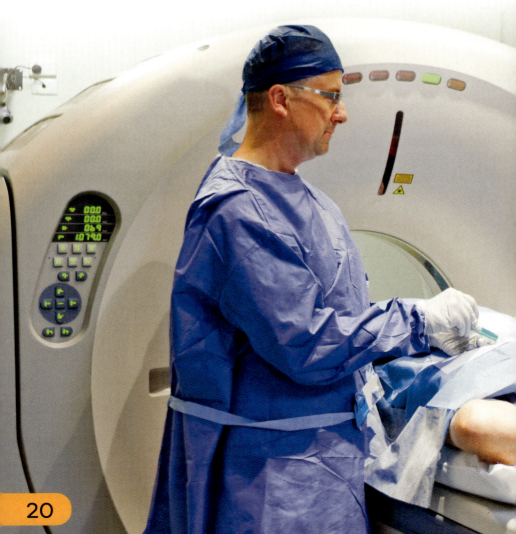

They do different jobs. They talk about how to help patients.

Working as a team means they can take care of lots of people.

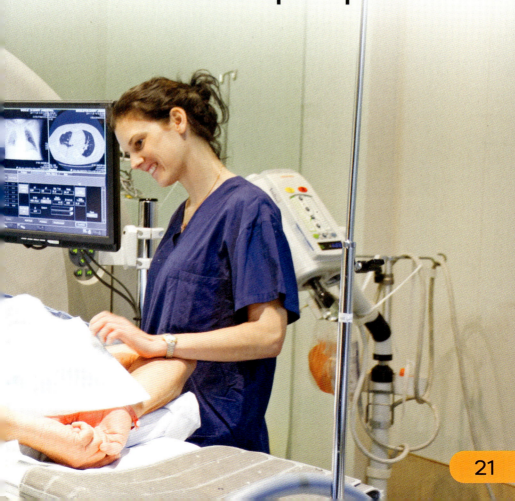

21

Staying Healthy

This girl is getting a checkup.

The doctor measures her height and weight. She listens to her heart and breathing. The doctor checks her ears and throat.

Next, the doctor gives her a shot. It hurts, but it is quick. There is medicine in the shot. It will help the girl stay healthy.

This girl fell off her bike. She hurt her arm. The doctor sends her to get an X-ray. An X-ray shows the bones inside her arm. The doctor sees that her arm is broken.

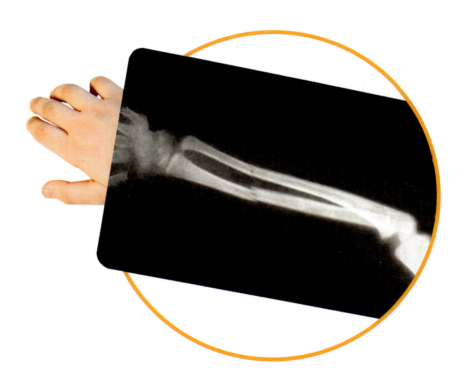

She puts a cast on her arm. The cast will hold the bones in place while they heal.

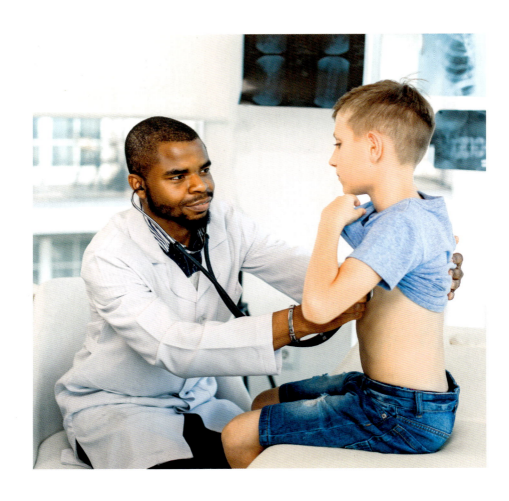

This boy isn't feeling well. The doctor figures out what is making him feel sick. This is called a diagnosis.

He sends a prescription to the pharmacy. The pharmacy will get medicine ready for him.

The medicine will help the boy feel better.

A Long Day

At the end of the day, the doctors look at test results. They add notes to their charts.

Sometimes, they call to check on patients.

Time to head home. Tomorrow will be another busy day!

Glossary

diagnosis
a doctor's understanding of what is making someone sick

prescription
an order for medicine from a doctor

primary care doctor
a doctor who keeps track of a person's overall health

scrubs
special clothes for doctors and nurses

stethoscope
a tool that lets a doctor hear sounds inside a person's body

Index

baby 15
blood pressure cuff 19
checkup 12, 22
clinic 12, 16
diagnosis 26
doing rounds 15
emergencies 16
field hospitals and clinics 16
hospital 14, 16, 17
medicine 23, 27
mobile hospitals 17

otoscope 19
patients 8, 9, 12, 15, 21, 29
prescription 27
primary care doctor 9
scrubs 11
stethoscope 18
teamwork 20, 21
thermometer 19
tongue depressor 19
tools 10, 18, 19
X-ray 24

Quiz

Answer the questions to see what you have learned. Check your answers with an adult.

1. Where do doctors work?
2. True or False: A person who is visiting the doctor is called a patient.
3. What is a cast used for?
4. Who are some people on a doctor's team?
5. True or False: A diagnosis is when a doctor determines what is causing a patient to feel bad.

1. At a clinic or hospital 2. True 3. Helping a broken bone heal 4. Nurses and other doctors 5. True